THE FLEXIB

CW00435146

RUN MORE AND W.

By

MIKAEL STOCKHOLM

Copyright © 2017

INTRODUCTION

Running is a very popular activity and sport. Many people throughout the world participate in running events all year round and whether they run every other day or only infrequently they are risking injury. Some runners use running to travel to see new cities and countries, but running can cause frequent injuries for some. Most running injuries require either expensive physiotherapy or a good deal of rest. I know, during my time running I have dealt with my own injuries, from groin strains, hamstrings and even torn calf muscles (ouch!).

For one injury I spent over $600 (~€550) on painful physiotherapy.

If you want to learn the secrets to my injury free (touch-wood) running techniques that have served me over the last few years then this book is for you. I hope you get something from it and more importantly I hope you avoid unnecessary injuries. You too could go from a couch Zero to a 10k Hero in no time.

I am not a medical expert or a Physio so don't expect to much medical mumbo jumbo here. All my tips are practical and have worked for me during training.

Not everyone is the same, therefore I would say that my techniques might not apply to everyone but they should apply to the majority of you.

The first couple of chapters outline my own experiences as a first time Runner. But those of you with a little more experience might get something from it.

TABLE OF CONTENTS

LEGAL NOTES

This is not a medically backed study or based on scientific facts. I am not medically trained or claim to be. The techniques are those found to work the best for me. Some of the reasoning for my use of certain techniques was based on science that I read about and tried for myself.

MY RUNNING HISTORY

I started running by accident. I was trying to get fit and did not think I was capable of running 5k without vast amounts of stamina building or training sessions. I attended martial arts classes twice a week and some Tae Bo classes twice a month, to lose weight and get fit. I then signed up to do a 5k run for charity thinking I would probably walk most of the way but jog for stretches at a time.

The run was two months away and I kept up my classes in the meantime. Martial arts classes can be great if the drills involve a lot of cardio and Tae Bo classes are amazing for your cardio. (Note: Any aerobic exercise can work just as well as Tae Bo – Boxercise or generic Aerobics class)

I was getting nervous and decided to do a treadmill run at the local gym to see how far I could run in one go. I thought I could maybe manage 10 minutes of running at jogging pace. I plugged in my iPod and put on my fast tracks and started running at 10km per hr speed.

Music does help and fast motivational music makes all the different to your willpower when trying to push on to reach that last kilometer or mile.

I would like venture off-track here and provide my Top 10 tracks.

MY TOP 10 RUNNING TRACKS FOR BLOKES (IN REVERSE ORDER)

10. Homeward Bound by Simon & Garfunkel – For when your past half-way and on the way home.

9. Rosanna by Toto – Feelgood song to lift the mood.

8. Road to Nowhere by Talkin Heads – Image from the video of Dave Byrne running as if on treadmill, immediately comes to mind. Good on ya Dave!

7. Nighttrain by Guns and Roses – Great song to move to.

6. Symphony of Destruction by Megadeath – Makes you feel indestructible. US army play this track inside their Tanks!

5. Paperback Writer by Beatles – Great song and takes your mind off the run while the lyrical absurdness makes you smile.

4. Centerfold by J. Geils Band – Sooo upbeat and a bit cheeky. Also brings you back to your schooldays.

3. Don't Stop Believin' by Journey – I am fan of Journey since before they were on the Sopranos. Plus a few years back I met Neal Schon in San Franciso.

2. Burn by Deep Purple – Coverdale and Hughes with an amazing song, which actually has a great story!

1. Eye of the Tiger by Survivor – Nothing moves you more and gets you fist-punching the air like this song.

Some of these are not my favourite Bands or songs, they are just my favourite running songs.

Add these and your own to a Running List consisting of 20 or so songs for your iPod.

Back to my treadmill run...I was completely lost in the music and didn't realise I just ran over the 5k limit and did a complete 28 minute session on the treadmill. The sweat was pouring out of me but I was smiling from ear to ear.

My first race

The race day for the charity event finally came. I was psyched up but confused about the amount of closes to wear. Sheeeeeesh! Decisions, decisions...will I be too warm, will I be too cold. In the end I wore an extra layer and decided if I got too warm running I would remove it and tie it around my waist. Problem solved!

For my first run I did not obey half of the list below and I only discovered them along the way by trial and error. I hope this list gives you a better head start than I had.

Top 10 Things To Bring Along for Races

10. Bandages / Plasters / Ice Spray or maybe even a small first aid kit. Falling hurts like hell!

9. Pouch or pocket or arm holder for phone keys and emergency Tenner (money).

8. Your timing chip / race number info etc. – Or you wont be allowed to run.

7. Gels / Tablets – Unless you just loaded up on slow burning carbs like pasta, you might find yourself losing energy fast or your legs getting weak. Gels are good but I find Dextrose (or Lucozade) energy tablets ideal to carry for a long run.

6. iPod / Mp3 – Unless the surroundings are fabulously beautiful, I get bored while running. It doesn't have a lot of brain stimulus to stop me from starting to feel bored. My motivational running tracks are needed. I now also listen to Podcasts I enjoy. More about this later.

5. Change of clothes (left in car or bagging area) – Towel. Thermal synthetic long sleeve top. Dry socks. Extra Underwear. Extra pair of shoes. Maybe a hot flask of tea or soup.

4. Hat / Cap / Gloves – Not everyone likes wearing caps or hats while running. I do NOT like the heat and the Sun just kills my will power and makes me sluggish, but with a cap I can get through it as the Sun in not beating down on my head. Similarly a cap or hat is good for cold or rainy weather. Some baldies like running in the rain with no cap / hat but I have hair

so I don't. Good on ya lads. Gloves are for colder runs – Duh!

3. Extra drinks / snacks – Most events give you water and snacks after you cross the finish line and water stops along the way for warm weather running. But you should bring your own too.

2. Running Shoes that suit you! In the next chapter I will discuss Shoes in detail as there is a fair bit involved.

1. Sunglasses – Nothing pisses me off more than running against the wind with the sun shining in your face, making you squint, and little kamikaze flies bouncing off your eyeballs. So do not forget the Shades or Sunnies or whatever you call them.

Even if its not sunny – if it rains it's much easier to run in the face-pelting rain with shades on – they be like your armour dude!

Now back the race. Once I arrived and got settled I was amazed at the amount of people that showed up and were about run. I did my warm-ups and stretching, or what I should say is, I copied everything everybody else was doing! Uh oh!

Later on you will find that I completely changed how I handle warm-ups and stretching.

You know it isn't just injuries that can stop you from running. Being ill or sick also prevents you from running or training. So the change of clothes helps avoid that. The sweat and bacteria collected after a run can give you a nasty cold if you do not shower soon after.

A friend of mine is really into his running and runs in all weathers – but he is often sick or sniffling with a cold! I think he's doing better now but I think the not showering after in time was a high factor.

TOP TIP: Shower within the Hour!

Not All Plain Sailing

After a week or two of running and doing the stuff I thought was right for me. I had a bit of an episode. While doing some light training of Tae Kwon Do one Saturday the instructor had lined us up do some sprints. After two I felt a small twinge in my leg but thought nothing of it.

After the third or fourth sprint I felt something painful like someone kicked my calf and thought I heard a pop! My calf was pulled (later I would find out it was also torn).

Jesus! The pain, the instructor and couple of the guys came over and gave me ice spray and tiger balm (fantastic stuff is that tiger balm! Shaolin Monks use it!)

I limped home and took a bath. In the bath I rang my local Physiotherapist. He said the swelling would be too bad to work on and that I do the RICE method. I slightly modified the method to be RICEL.

Rest – Lots of it! Stay off the leg!

Ice – Ice packs or frozen peas and ice sprays every few hours after the incident and over the next two days.

Compression – Wrap a tight bandage around it but not so tight that it is uncomfortable or cutting off blood supply to the area.

Elevation – Keep the leg up and raised higher than your hips.

Lie Back – And watch a TV Boxset / Netflix show you kept putting off! Very important otherwise you will not stay easy and you will use any excuse to get up.

Most anti-inflammatory over the counter tablets are fine and help but seek medical advice before you take anything.

The therapy was very painful but necessary, the tear formed a knot in my calf muscle and needed to be worked out. About 12 sessions worth! Each one involved tears and loud wailing.

I was giving a series of stretching exercises for my calves to lengthen and strengthen the damaged leg.

So what did I learn form that episode is the cold sprints are bad for me, very bad!

I now try to avoid all fast sprinting if I can, it doesn't mean I can never run fast, just not from a cold start. So running and warming up the legs and getting blood flowing before building up speed. That's the ticket!

RUNNING SHOES AND GEAR

SHOES

Okay the most important part of your equipment to be concerned with. Your feet need to in the right shoes.

Step 1 - Get a Gait Test carried out.

You can get these at most good sports clothing outlets. They should have a test treadmill and motion capture camera to analyse your Gait when you run.

Gaits are not perfect and you need to be aware of the shop trying to sell you the latest and greatest pair of shoes.

Good shoes need to feel good on while just standing still.

If required you may need cushioning for a more comfortable run.

If you have arched feet or are flat-footed you will require special insoles for the shoes. These insoles can cost a lot of money but if you need them, then you need them!!

A good way to get an indication of your feet type is to step out of the shower or bath with a wet foot and stand on the floor. Then take your foot up and look at the wet mark left.

Normal / Medium Arch

If you have thin area of wet on outer side of your mid foot area connecting the top and bottom section then you are most likely an average foot type and can use most shoes.

Flat / Low Arch

If most of the mid section is the roughly the same width when connecting between top and bottom parts of the feet then you most likely have flat feet and require some arch support from special shoes or insoles.

High Arch

If you see only the heel and the ball of your foot then you have a high arch. This usually means a well-cushioned shoe with no extra arch insole support is required.

Finding your ideal shoe is a matter of trial and error but your advisor at the store should be able to provide with good options and also request doing a short run on their treadmill to see if the shoe feels good when running.

Be mindful of the impact of the shoes, if the feel like they have enough suspension or cushioning to suit you and try to gauge if your knees or hips are feeling anything when you run.

Other things to look out for...

If you plan to run in a lot of bad weather make sure the shoe is waterproof or water resistant. The Nike Pegasus range is an example of one such shoe.

CLOTHES

Okay we will keep this short – Cotton is a no-no. Synthetics and quick drying items made for good absorption are required here.

Cold weather – Wear something that is wind resistant but breathable over your running top. A running garment with an elasticated V opening at the top with a hood is great. If you get too hot pull your arms out of your sleeves and pull the V down your waist now the top is only around your waist and if you get cold again you can easily pull it back up – all without interfering in your run as you wont need to stop. But keep your eyes on the road!

Socks – Thin sport socks with quick drying ability which also do not sweat your feet. Make sure your feet do not slide about inside your shoes or you will get blisters.

Arm bands – I use weatherproof armband case to carry my phone and iPod. You can hold it in your hands if you prefer but the case is great protection against falling or dropping it.

My warm-ups and warm-downs

Okay here is the thing – I have had really bad injuries from stretching too much before a run!

Sounds crazy, right? It's true and there is a scientific reason for it.

You see stretching the muscles and tendons while the body is in a normal relatively inactive or cold state can cause injuries and put strain on your body.

I do not stretch at all before running! And it works great for me!

So what do I do instead, I do a gentle warm-up instead. I start a slow jog on flat ground or the treadmill at a pace of 6km / hr for about two minutes. After that I bump the speed up to 9 or 10 km / hr then gradually more after a few minutes.

You may find this works great for you, and if you only get at least one useful takeaway from this book then it will be worth it.

You might have seen them at running events, the announcer over P.A. system shouting for you to warm up and jump around and stretch out your legs. I would be careful about following the 'Horde' on this. Do your own thing, everyone is different and this group-warm mentality is not ideal for everyone.

If you notice your calves acting up or giving you signals your in pain at any stage during your run, you should slow down and take it slower. If the pain is nagging and constant then stop, you might have a slight strain and may need to take things a bit slower. You may need to build some more strength and stamina into your legs.

You calf muscles will build-up over time and you will get more and more used to running without extensive stretching.

Now although I said I do not stretch before the run, but I do shortly afterwards. I will go in to that soon too.

For a warm down, once your distance or time goal is reached, just reduce the speed of the treadmill back down the 6km / hr setting and fast-walk at this speed for approx. 2 minutes.

If you are at home on a treadmill then you should have a shower, if on a run then you can walk a bit longer (5 minutes).

After your shower or walk you should start to stretch out those hamstrings and calf muscles.

FIGURE 1.

Stretch arm on leg toes down grabbing near the ankle

FIGURE 2.

Arms on leg grabbing foot - toes up and slowly bend forearm inline with your leg (touching your leg).

Repeat again for other leg.

FIGURE 3.

Arm against a wall for balance. Grab leg behind you. Keep back straight and pull you foot back to your buttocks.

Repeat for the other leg.

Also, if you are unused to running and are feeling especially sore over the next day or so I would also recommend getting hold of some Epsom Salts. Three to four hand or cup-fulls of Epsom Salts into a nice hot bath will do a lot for sore leg muscles. Soak for about 30 – 40 minutes. Also helps provide a great nights sleep.

BEATING THE BOREDOM

Some runners would disagree with me, but I am sure I am not the only one that enjoys the run and the feeling afterwards, but also find the activity a little boring.

Unless your running in fabulous surroundings or with a friend you will probably get a little bored from time to time.

Register for a Race!!

If you are registered you know you have to run the race and this in itself is a great motivator for getting your training on track. Give yourself enough time and register for a race that is at least two months away.

Book a Flight!

Find a race in another city or even in another country. Then book your flights and hotel and start training for it! You will now have another running goal set and also a short holiday trip to look forward to. Running tourism is very popular and it is very big in Europe where many short races, half and full marathons take place all year round in various stunning city locations.

Some of the popular European running destinations are:

- Barcelona, Spain
- Paris, France
- Budapest, Hungary
- Dublin, Ireland
- London, England

Plus many, many, more.

A cheaper way to beat that boredom is have various routes to run in your local area. I often run in Central Park or other park / woodland areas. I also travel to remote locations to do some running away from the hustle and bustle of city life.

I mentioned earlier that running tracks are great for motivation but they too can become boring if you are over-exposed to them. Other items that can help this are Podcasts. I love listening to my favourite Podcasts during a run, and they are great for creating an incentive to get you committed to doing the run, whereas the music tracks create the desire and willpower to continue and slog through the pain towards the end of a run.

With Podcasts, everyone will have their own favourites, because they are created around various topics and hobbies. There is literally something for everyone and once your start listening to Podcasts, you might become addicted to them.

Some examples of Podcasts – all of which are 100% free! You can find Podcasts on iTunes, Stitcher, Playstore etc.

- Sport – Choose your favourite sport. Although avoid 'Golf' Podcasts unless you want your boredom to go off the chart!! Find a sport podcast (apart from Golf) and enjoy!

- Business – Lots of great Podcasts around the business and entrepreneur world. One of my favourites is the STARTUP PODCAST by Gimlet Media.

- Gaming – Video gamers of you will be able to listen to fun banter about video game news on the all the consoles.

- Films and TV – Great podcasts on the newest films and TV shows.

Gimlet Media have a number of fabulous podcasts, covering various topics, all of which are professionally produced, and all of which, keep you entertained for many a long run.

Audiobooks

Another excellent way to keep the interest up is listening to great audio books by your favourite authors. These are not free but they are well worth the money if you can find books that interest you and that keep you engaged.

Audiobooks not only have to be good books and well written but the narrative style and voice of the audio narrator needs to be to your taste also.

Here are some examples of great audiobooks with great narrators.

- I Am Legend by Richard Mattheson read by Robertson Dean (My favourite)

- Just Kids by Patti Smith read by Patti Smith

- Salem's Lot by Stephen King read by Ron McLarty

- Steve Jobs by Walter Isaacson ready by Dylan Baker

FLEXIBILITY STRETCHING WORKOUT

I mentioned earlier that I came from a Martial Arts background. Well that's where this section goes into more detail on the main exercises that have made my running activities so injury free.

As a daily routine, if you have some time and a bit of floor space you can do the following set of stretches to help with the strain in your legs. These stretches, some similar to those of Yoga are excellent. You can do them in the afternoon or evening, I avoid doing these stretches in the morning as your muscles are very stiff then. It's better to do them after any runs that day. So do not do this stretching routine before your daily or regular run.

This stretching routine helps with general health too and builds up muscle in your hamstrings and calves. Thus making your muscles less susceptible to injury overall.

Some optional equipment you might consider for this activity...

- A strong belt or stretching band or resistance band or martial arts belt. My preference is a belt called FlexFixx Stretch belt, which you can find on Amazon.

- A Yoga mat if your surface floor area is slippy or rough.

- Bare feet or Footwear that will not slide along the floor when stretching.

- Timer on your smartphone.

Once again we are concerned with building heat into the muscles and getting blood flowing so as not to pull or strain anything from a cold start.

I have two go to exercises for this...

Exercise 1 – The Horse Stance – Origin of the horse stance comes from Chinese Martial arts or Kung Fu and builds strength in the legs.

Sit in the horse stance for a short period at the start – 20 seconds, building up over time to up to 3 – 4 minutes

Keep your back and neck straight. Make sure your knees do not go past your toes...Keep them inline with your ankles.

Keep you bum and back inline.

After a while you can lower your thighs to be more inline with your knees but this is a much more intense stretch.

After you come out of the horse stance give your legs a little shake to loosen them up.

Exercise 2 – The Wall Sit

Another great strength exercise for your thighs and hamstrings.

Again this is a slow build up so start with only 20 seconds and build up to 2 minutes (2 minutes is a killer in this stretch!)

If you feel pain or discomfort you can stand back up out of the stretch. You may find this hard at first and feel a bit of stress on you

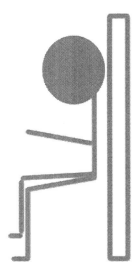

You keep your back against the wall or a closed door (making sure no one will open it suddenly of course!)

A bit like the horse stance but this one works different muscles and it a lot tougher.

Now we get to the rest of the stretches.

Each of these can be held for up to 20 seconds at the start working gradually up to about 1 minute or so.

I tend to do repetitions of each for 30 to 40 seconds but you can do whatever works best for you.

FIGURE 1 – ONE LEGGED SQUAT STRETCH

On your toes squat to one side and keep the other leg straight. Hold for 20 to 30 seconds and repeat for other leg.

FIGURE 2 HURDLERS STRETCH OR HAMSTRING STRETCH

Try to grab your toes or ankle or knee and try to bring your head down to your knee of the extended leg with your other leg bent and pressed against you extended leg. Hold for 30 seconds if possible.

Repeat for other leg.

Note on breathing: Like Yoga breathing is important in some of these stretches. Breathe in before engaging in the stretch then breathe out slowly while stretching and feeling the burn. In through the nose and out through the mouth.

FIGURE 3 – SITTING SPLITS

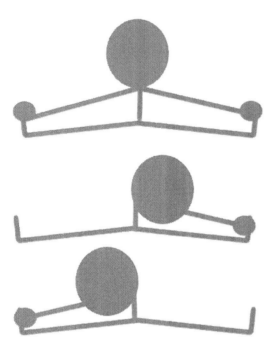

As you can see sit on the floor and lift each of your buttocks up once to allow for a better stretch. Spread your legs wide but not too wide to be uncomfortable.

Grab both toes or ankles or knees and hold for 30 – 40 seconds.

Then do again and bring your head down to your knee while grabbing toes, ankle or knee with both hands. Hold for 20 seconds (work up to it maybe start with 5 seconds).

Don't forget to breathe.

Now repeat Exercise 2 and see if the stretch is easier.

Then repeat this exercise.

FIGURE 4 – FORWARD BEND IN SPLITS

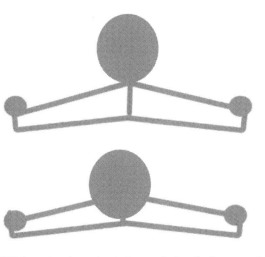

Sitting in the stretch grab both feet or legs below the knee then slowly bring your body forward. This one takes time to build up. Its quick hard at first. Eventually you will be able to bring your head to the floor. Each time breathe in and hold and breathe out when extending your stretch.

FIGURE 5 – SHAKE OUT

Bring your legs in slowly together and out straight in front of you then shake them out and rotate your feet about the ankles etc.

Shake out your calves and hamstrings.

20 to 40 seconds.

FIGURE 6 – BUTTERFLY STRETCH

Sitting in a post like from a Yoga seated position. Grab your two feet and rest your elbows on your knees.

Ever so slightly add pressure to the knees using your elbows and feel the stretch on the inside of your thighs.

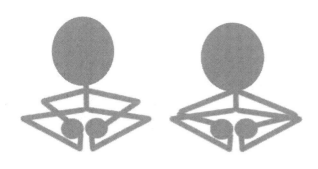

Again hold for 30 seconds and release. Repeat for 3 more times.

Stretch out your legs like before and shake them out again. Now using your arms slowly turn to your side and bring your self back up standing.

Once you are up give your legs another shake out and that's it.

That's a basic Flexibility Stretch Workout for you to do every day not just on running days.

I guarantee you will feel the benefits of these stretches after 3 weeks and you will become addicted to them because they will strengthen your legs and reduce injuries from running as a result.

Thanks for purchasing this book and giving the time to learn something new!

Please leave a nice review.

Updated content with more detailed stretching will be added in the near future.

Thanks a lot,

Mikael Stockholm

ABOUT THE AUTHOR

Mikael Stockholm is an entrepreneur living and sport running fanatic originally from Sweden but who now lives in New York in USA.

OTHER BOOKS BY (AUTHOR)

Currently writing a more detailed book on running.

Can I Ask A Favor?

If you enjoyed this book, found it useful or otherwise then I'd really appreciate it if you would post a short review on Amazon. I do read all the reviews personally so that I can continually write what people are wanting.

If you'd like to leave a review then please visit the link below:

https://www.amazon.com/Flexible-Runner-injuries-stretching-injury-free-ebook/dp/B0714PRH5C/

Thanks for your support!

Printed in Great Britain
by Amazon

68233031R00028